Body Coverings

Fur

Cassie Mayer

www.heinemann.co.uk/library
Visit our website to find out more information about **Heinemann Library** books.

To order:
☎ Phone 44 (0) 1865 888066
▤ Send a fax to 44 (0) 1865 314091
▣ Visit the Heinemann Bookshop at www.heinemann.co.uk/library to browse our catalogue and order online.

First published in Great Britain by Heinemann Library, Halley Court, Jordan Hill, Oxford OX2 8EJ, part of Harcourt Education. Heinemann is a registered trademark of Harcourt Education Ltd.

Editorial: Tracey Crawford, Cassie Mayer, Dan Nunn, and Sarah Chappelow
Design: Jo Hinton-Malivoire
Picture Research: Tracy Cummins
Production: Duncan Gilbert

Originated by Chroma Graphics (Overseas) Pte. Ltd
Printed and bound in China by South China Printing Company

10 digit ISBN 0 431 18280 9
13 digit ISBN 978 0 431 18280 3

10 09 08 07 06
10 9 8 7 6 5 4 3 2 1

British Library Cataloguing in Publication Data
Mayer, Cassie
Fur. – (Body coverings)
1.Fur – Juvenile literature 2.Fur-bearing animals – Juvenile literature I.Title
599.7'147

Acknowledgements
The publishers would like to thank the following for permission to reproduce photographs:
Corbis pp. **6** (Paul A. Souders), **11** and **12** (Nigel J. Dennis/Gallo Images), **13** (Jones), **14** (Wolfe), **15** and **16** (Kevin Schafer/zefa), **18** (Martin Harvey), **20** (Kevin Dodge), **22** (cat, Pat Doyle), **23** (porcupine, Nigel J. Dennis/Gallo Images); Flpa p. **22** (wild boar); Getty Images pp. **7** and **8** (Warden), **9**, **10** and **23** (sheep, Miller); Getty Images/Digital Vision pp. **4** (kingfisher and rhino), **5** (cheetah), **23** (cheetah); Getty Images/PhotoDisc pp. **4** (snail and lizard), **17**, **23** (giraffe); Nature Picture Library p. **22** (lion, Christophe Courteau).

Cover photograph of tiger fur, reproduced with permission of William Dow/Corbis. Back cover image of bear fur reproduced with permission of Warden/Getty Images.

Special thanks to the Smithsonian Institution and Jonathan Ballou for their help with this project.

Every effort has been made to contact copyright holders of any material reproduced in this book. Any omissions will be rectified in subsequent printings if notice is given to the publishers.

The paper used to print this book comes from sustainable resources.

Contents

feathers

shell

scales

skin

All animals have body coverings.
Look at these body coverings.

fur

This animal has fur.
Fur is a body covering too.

There are different types of fur.

Fur can be thick.
What animal is this?

This animal is a bear.
Its thick fur keeps it warm.

Fur can be curly.
What animal is this?

This animal is a sheep.
Its curly fur is called wool.

Fur can be sharp.
What animal is this?

quills

This animal is a porcupine.
Its sharp fur is called quills.

Fur can be soft and fluffy.
What animal is this?

baby cheetah

This animal is a baby cheetah.
Its fluffy fur changes when it grows.

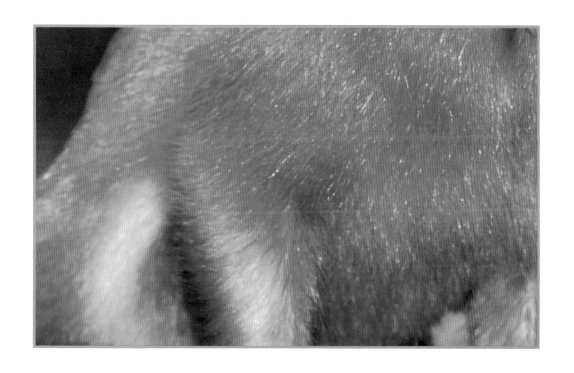

Fur can be bright colours.
What animal is this?

This animal is a monkey.
Its bright fur helps it to be seen.

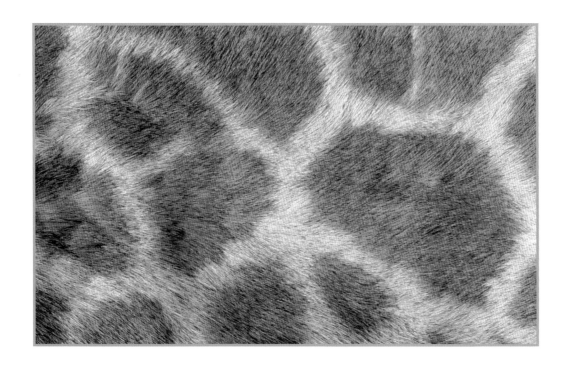

Fur can have patterns.
What animal is this?

This animal is a giraffe.
Its fur helps it to hide.

Do you have fur?

Yes! You have fur!
Your fur is called hair.

Fur quiz

(answers on page 24)

1. I live in a field.
    My fur is curly.
    My fur is called wool.
    What am I?

2. My fur is sharp.
    My fur is called quills.
    The quills help to protect me.
    What am I?

Fun fur facts

Sometimes fur stands up straight when animals are scared.

A lion's mane makes a lion look fierce.

Wild boars have fur that protects them from mud.

Picture glossary

 **fur** a type of body covering

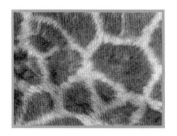 **pattern** an arrangement of markings. Patterns on fur help animals to hide.

 **quill** sharp fur. Quills help to protect porcupines.

 **wool** curly fur. A sheep's fur is called wool.

Index

Notes to parents and teachers

Before reading
Talk about how animals have different body coverings – fur, feathers, shells, scales, and skin. Talk about the different kinds of fur – some fur is thick (bear, dog), some fur is curly (sheep), some fur is soft (kitten, baby cheetah), and some fur can even be sharp (hedgehog spines and porcupine quills). Talk about how fur helps animals to keep warm and protects them from enemies.

After reading
Collect examples of different body coverings – fun fur, feathers, shells. (Make scales by drawing scales on to cardboard and scoring the lines). Encourage children to describe the textures and colours. Put the body coverings in a "feely box" and challenge children to identify them. Cut out pictures of animals and help children sort them into the different body coverings. Draw an outline of a bear, a sheep, and a hedgehog. Help the children to make a collage using fun fur, white or black wool, and cardboard drinking straws.

Answers to quiz: 1. I am a sheep. 2. I am a porcupine.

Titles in the *Body Coverings* series include:

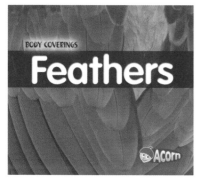

Hardback   0 431 18281 7

Hardback   0 431 18279 5

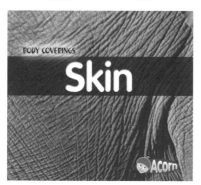

Hardback   0 431 18282 5

Hardback   0 431 18280 9

Hardback   0 431 18278 7

Find out about other titles from Heinemann Library on our website www.heinemann.co.uk/library